TABLE OF CONTENTS

MW00452235

Mocktails*

Watermelon Fennel Mint

500 g WATERMELON
100 g FENNEL
5 g FRESH MINT
7 ICE CUBES

→ BLEND TILL FROTHY
SERVE IMMEDIATELY

Pomegranate Ice Tea

500 ML HERBAL TEA, COOLED
300 ML POMEGRANATE JUICE
1 PIECE ORGANIC LIME PEEL

→ MIX AND SERVE OVER ICE

Strawberry Daiquiri

250 g STRAWBERRIES
350 ML WATER KEFIR
2 TBSP LIME JUICE
HONEY TO TASTE
3 CUPS OF ICE

→ BLEND IN MIXER
SERVE IMMEDIATELY

Indian Orange

350 ML FRESH ORANGE
JUICE
100 ML ALMOND MILK
1/4 TSP GARAM MASALA

→ BLEND IN MIXER
SERVE IMMEDIATELY

HERBAL TEA &

thyme + sage

lemon + ginger

peppermint & lemon balm

Cinnamon
HOT CHOCOLATE

Mix 1 TSP of cocoa powder, 1 TSP honey and 1/4 TSP cinnamon with 4 TSP cream in a cup. Add boiling water and stir. Enjoy with cookies.

OLIVE OIL WITH HERBS + SPICES

CHILI

BASIL

GARLIC

ROSEMARY

OREGANO

ORANGE PEEL

Place dried herbs in the bottom of a bottle. Pour olive oil over the herbs. Let it infuse for several weeks.

OLIVE TAPENADE

DIRECTIONS

Mince 3 cloves garlic in a food processor, add 200 g pitted kalamata olives, 2 TSP capers, 3 TSP fresh parsley, 2 TSP lemon juice, 2 TSP olive oil and blend until everything is chopped. Season to taste with salt and pepper.

Pesto
RED + GREEN

Making pesto is easy: chop all the ingredients and place everything (except cheese + olive oil) into a small mixer or a pestle and mortar. Grind to a coarse paste. Stir in the cheese and olive oil and adjust the seasoning to taste.

Red: 100g dried tomatoes, 40g cashews, 2 cloves garlic, 40g parmesan, 130 ml olive oil, salt + chili

Green: 2 big bunches of basil, 130 ml olive oil, 2 cloves garlic, 60g pine nuts, 60g parmesan, salt

Bruschetta

Cut a baguette in 1cm slices and toast in a pan until golden. Rub gently with a clove of garlic and drizzle olive oil over it. Top with a mix of diced tomatoes, basil, vinegar, salt and pepper. If you want variation to the classic recipe, add cheese or herbs or marinated veggies.

Arugula
Orange
Salad

Place
4 cups arugula and
2 oranges, peeled + cut into
segments, into a bowl. Drizzle with
4 Ts olive oil, and 2 Ts balsamic vinegar,
then sprinkle with salt. Top
with almond halves.
Toss + Serve.

Romaine & Pear Salad

Place torn pieces of one head of romaine lettuce, 2 shredded carrots and one sliced spring onion in a bowl and toss. Roast 3 tbsp of sunflower seeds until golden. Garnish the salad with sunflower seeds and 2 diced pears. Whisk together ¼ cup vinegar, ½ tsp salt, a dash of pepper, ½ tsp mustard and 1 tsp honey. Blend in ½ cup olive oil until combined and pour over salad.

ASPARAGUS SOUP

500 g white asparagus

1 L veggie broth

2 cloves garlic, peeled

50 g butter

juice of 1 lemon

1 cup heavy cream

4 TBSP flour

salt + nutmeg

Trim 1/2 cm from the asparagus ends, then peel the stalks. Cut into 3 cm pieces. Boil the veggie broth, add garlic and asparagus and simmer for 10 min. Add butter, lemon juice, salt and nutmeg to taste. Remove the garlic. Mix flour and cream and add both into the soup. Simmer for one minute and serve. Garnish with spicy cress or dandelion.

Tom Ka Tofu

Ingredients

1 can coconut milk
500 ml vegetable broth
2 stalks lemongrass (cut into pieces)
2 inches fresh ginger
150 g broccoli florets
1 medium zucchini

½ red bell pepper
3-4 oyster mushrooms
2 tbs. soy sauce
1 tbs. honey
6 kaffir lime leaves
150 g cubed tofu

Directions

1. Boil vegetable broth + coconut milk. Add lemongrass + ginger, simmer 10 minutes. Strain through a mesh, return liquid to saucepan.
2. Add the rest of the ingredients (veggies cut into fine slices or discs) and cook for 10 minutes.
3. Remove lime leaves, and serve with rice.

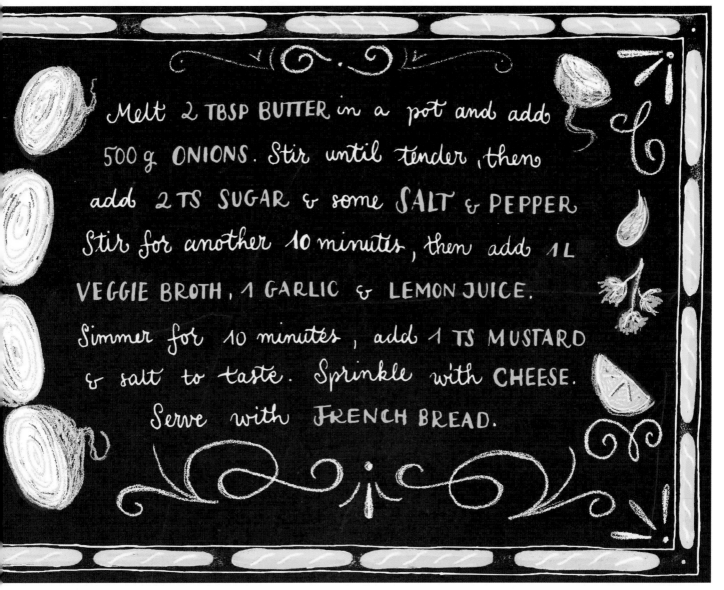

Melt 2 TBSP BUTTER in a pot and add 500 g ONIONS. Stir until tender, then add 2 TS SUGAR & some SALT & PEPPER Stir for another 10 minutes, then add 1 L VEGGIE BROTH, 1 GARLIC & LEMON JUICE. Simmer for 10 minutes, add 1 TS MUSTARD & salt to taste. Sprinkle with CHEESE. Serve with FRENCH BREAD.

Oven roasted Veggies

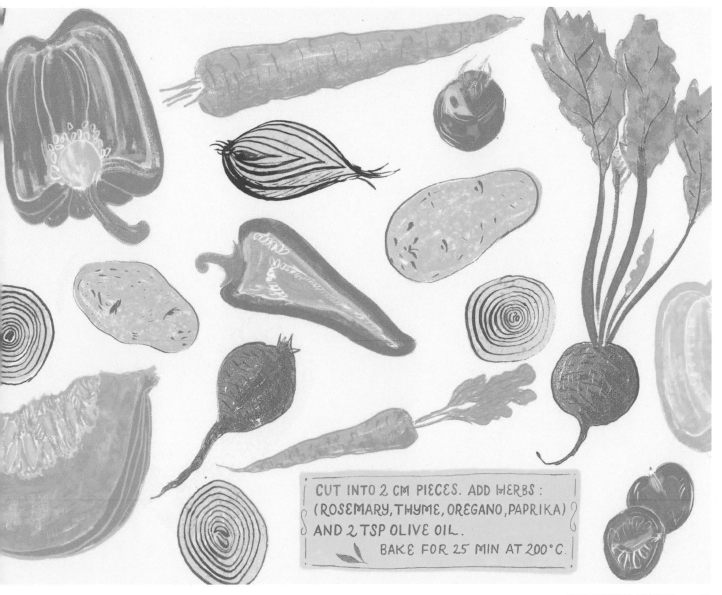

CUT INTO 2 CM PIECES. ADD HERBS :
(ROSEMARY, THYME, OREGANO, PAPRIKA)
AND 2 TSP OLIVE OIL.
BAKE FOR 25 MIN AT 200°C.

①.
Wash 5 potatoes, and cut them in wedges. Spread on a baking tray. Sprinkle with olive oil, salt + paprika. Bake at 200°C for 20 min.

②
In the meantime grate the cucumber and stir it into 1 cup of sour cream. Season with herbs, salt + pepper, and serve with the potatoes.

POTATO WEDGES

WITH CUCUMBER DIP

Mix 150 g spelt flour, 50 g soy flour, 1 pinch of salt, 1 TSP of baking soda, 350 ml water and let it sit for 10 minutes. Heat 1 TSP of coconut oil in a pan and pour some of the mix in it and cook for a few minutes. Flip and cook until golden. Keep the pancakes warm as you make the rest. Serve with sliced bananas, blueberries and maple syrup.

BANANA PANCAKES

Dandelion Quiche

Mix 250 g whole wheat flour, 1 TSP TSP salt and 100 g butter until they're crumbly. Add 3 TBSP water and form a dough that you spread into a form with baking paper. Cut 2 handful of dandelion and 500 g leek into 2 cm pieces and cook them for 10 minutes with a bit of water. Add 200 g sour cream, salt and spices, pour into the form and bake for 30 min at 200 °C.

PIZZA FUNGHI

Make a dough from the yeast, water, flour, salt + oil. Let it rest in a warm place for 45 min. Roll out on a baking tray, then add the toppings: first the tomatoes, then the herbs + salt, mushrooms and finally the cheese. Put into the preheated oven (225°C) + bake for 15 min.

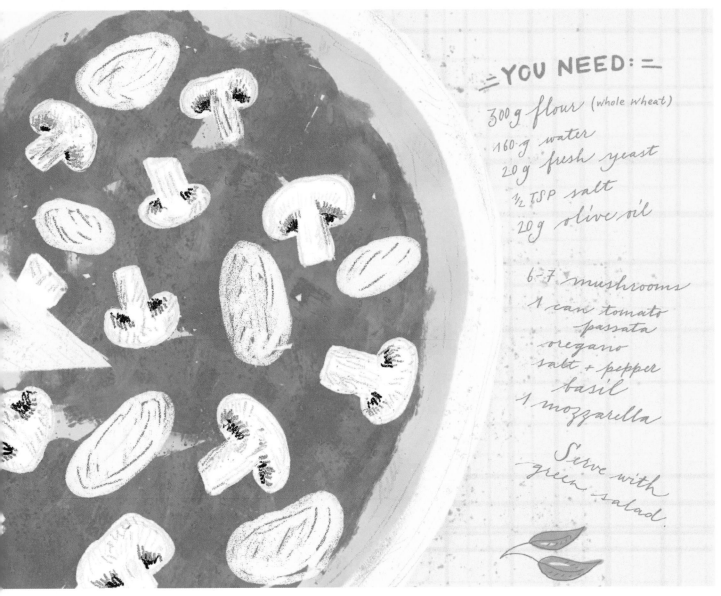

YOU NEED:

300 g flour (whole wheat)
160 g water
20 g fresh yeast
½ TSP salt
20 g olive oil

6-7 mushrooms
1 can tomato
     passata
oregano
salt + pepper
basil
1 mozzarella

Serve with
green salad.

Falafel

MASH 2 CANS OF CHICKPEAS.
ADD ONE DICED ONION, 2 TBSP
PARSLEY, ONE DICED CLOVE GARLIC,
3-4 TBSP FLOUR, AND CORIANDER, CHILI,
SALT + PEPPER TO TASTE. FORM SMALL
BALLS AND PUT ON A BAKING TRAY.
DRIZZLE WITH OLIVE OIL AND BAKE FOR
20-25 MINUTES. UNTIL GOLDEN.
SERVE WITH GUACAMOLE / RED
DIP / PITA BREAD AND FRESH
TOMATOES + CUCUMBER.

Guacamole

MASH 1 RIPE AVOCADO AND
MIX WITH LEMON JUICE,
SALT, PEPPER AND CHILI TO
TASTE. ADD CUBED TOMATOES.

Red Pepper Dip

DICE ONE RED BELL PEPPER,
ONE ONION AND ONE CLOVE GARLIC.
FRY WITH OLIVE OIL FOR 5 MIN.
ADD 1 CAN OF TOMATO PASSATA,
3 TBSP VINEGAR, 1 TBSP HONEY,
SALT + CHILI. SIMMER FOR 20 MIN.

DIRECTIONS

Cut one LEEK in 2cm increments. Heat 1 ts olive oil + stir the leek in it for 3 min. Add 1 cup of RED LENTILS + stir for another minute. Add 4 CUPS OF WATER and a pinch of SALT. Cook for 10 min. Add the JUICE OF ½ LEMON and 1 FRESH CHILI, chopped in small pieces. Decorate with PARSLEY and (VEGAN) SOUR CREAM. *ENJOY!*

CREAMY Farfalle WITH SPINACH

BOIL 150g Farfalle AL DENTE. IN THE MEAN TIME STEW 250g Spinach IN A PAN. ADD 4 TBSP OF (vegan) cream, salt, pepper & nutmeg. DRAIN THE PASTA & ADD IT TO THE SPINACH. DRIZZLE 1 TS olive oil OVER IT AND MIX EVERYTHING CAREFULLY. SERVE IMMEDIATELY.

PASTA
alla norma

Chop 1 aubergine in cubes, sprinkle with salt and set aside for 15 minutes. Peel 1 clove of garlic and slice ½ bunch of basil. Pat the aubergine dry, place into a heated pan with olive oil. Fry for 5-8 minutes. Add the garlic, basil, and 1 TSP capers. Cook for 2 minutes, then add a can of tomatoes. Simmer for 15 minutes. Cook as many wholewheat spaghetti as you need until 'al dente' and serve with sauce, pecorino and basil.

VEGETARIANA

Peas

Herbs & Onion

Lemon

Veggie

Broth

Heat 2 TSP olive oil in a deep pan, add 250g brown rice + 1 onion. Stir for 5 min and add 1 garlic, ¾ L broth and lemon peel, salt + pepper. Arrange 500g leek, 100g peas, 1 bell pepper and 75g black olives on the rice + cook with a lid on for 45 min. Decorate with lemon wedges + parsley and serve in the pan.

DIRECTIONS:

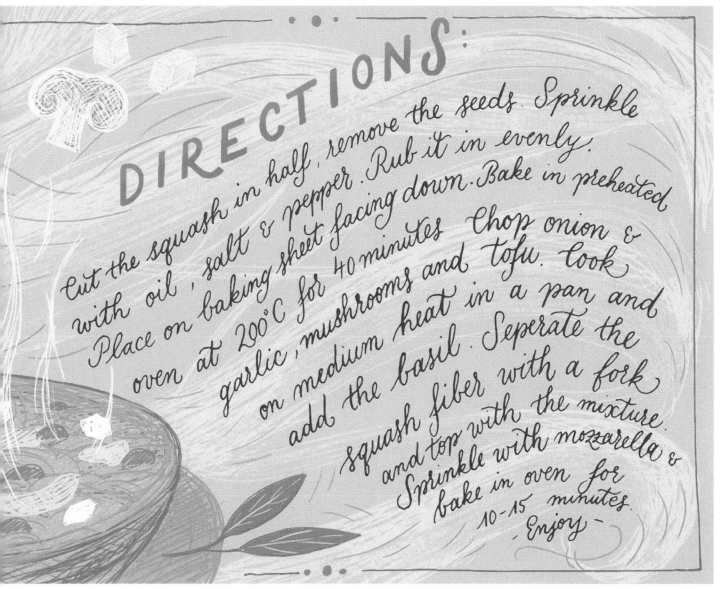

Cut the squash in half, remove the seeds. Sprinkle with oil, salt & pepper. Rub it in evenly. Place on baking sheet facing down. Bake in preheated oven at 200°C for 40 minutes. Chop onion & garlic, mushrooms and tofu. Cook on medium heat in a pan and add the basil. Seperate the squash fiber with a fork and top with the mixture. Sprinkle with mozzarella & bake in oven for 10-15 minutes.
- Enjoy -

MIX DIFFERENT FRUIT IN A BLENDER. ADD HONEY, CREAM OR FRUIT JUICE TO TASTE, POUR INTO POPSICLE MOLDS + FREEZE UNTIL IT'S FIRM. ENJOY!

POPSICLES

Apple Crumble

2-3 apples

Directions:

1. Cut the apples in slices.
2. Put the rest of ingredients in a bowl and mix into a crumbly batter.
3. Put the apples into a baking dish and the crumble mixture on top. Press gently together.
4. Bake for 20-25 min at 180°C until the top is golden.

50 g oats

FLOUR

125g flour

50 g honey

50 g butter

40 g sunflower seeds + almonds

Strawberry Trifle

PLACE ALL INGREDIENTS FOR THE
CRUMBLE IN A BOWL AND MIX. PUT ON
A BAKING TRAY WITH PAPER AND
BAKE FOR 12 MIN AT 200 G. LET IT COOL.
CUT THE STRAWBERRIES IN PIECES.

WHISK THE CREAM AND THE VANILLA,
THEN ADD YOGHURT, CURD AND HONEY.
PUT CRUMBLES, STRAWBERRIES
AND CREAM INTO A DESSERT BOWL
IN LAYERS.

FOR THE CRUMBLE :
175 G WHOLE WHEAT FLOUR
100 G HONEY
1 TS GROUND VANILLA
1 PINCH OF SALT
100 G SOFT BUTTER

FOR THE CREAM :
200 G CREAM
½ TS GROUND VANILLA
300 G YOGHURT
200 G CURD
40 G HONEY

750 G STRAWBERRIES

selfmade

chocolate

Melt 50 g cacao butter, 10 g coconut oil, 15 g cacao and 30 g honey. Add 40 g almond butter and mix well. Pour into chocolate molds and decorate with nuts, raisins, cacao or coconut shreds.

vegan CHEESE CAKE with berries

HONEY

CRUST:

200 g freshly milled flour, 100 g coconut oil, 50 g honey, 1 pinch of salt, 3-4 TBSP of water

Combine the flour with the coconut oil, add honey, salt and water and make a crumbly mixture. Put in the fridge for 30 minutes & then make a pie crust in a small round form (26 cm).

FILLING:

100 g coconut oil, 100 g honey, 500 g soy joghurt, 60 g rice flour, juice of half a lemon, 1 pinch of salt, 120 ml aqua faba (chickpea can liquid)

Combine all the dry ingredients (not the aqua faba) into a smooth mixture. Whisk the aqua faba seperately in a bowl until it's stiff. Add the aqua faba to the filling, carefully combine and fill into the form. Bake for: 60 min at 180°C

THEY DRAW & COOK™

Fresh & Fabulous Vegetarian
by Julia Bausenhardt

Copyright © 2017 Studio SSS, LLC
All rights reserved, including the
right of reproduction in whole or in
part in any form.

Conceived, designed and produced
by Studio SSS and
Julia Bausenhardt

STUDIO SSS, LLC
Nate Padavick & Salli Swindell
studiosss.com

JULIA BAUSENHARDT
juliabausenhardt.com

Conversions

Common Measurement Equivalents

3 TS = 1 TBS = 1/2 FL OZ
2 TS = 1 FL OZ
4 TS = 2 FL OZ = 1/4 C
8 TBS = 4 FL OZ = 1/2 C
16 TBS = 8 FL OZ = 1 C
16 FL OZ = 2 C = 1 PT
32 FL OZ = 4 C = 2 PT = 1 QT
128 FL OZ = 16 C = 8 PT = 4 QT = 1 G

Volume

1 TS	5 ML
1 TBS	15 ML
1/4 C	59 ML
1 C	236 ML
1 PT	472 ML
1 QT	944 ML
1 G	3.8 L

Length

1 IN	2.54 CM
4 IN	10 CM
6 IN	5 CM
8 IN	20 CM
9 IN	23 CM
10 IN	25 CM
12 IN	30 CM
13 IN	33 CM

Weight/Mass

1/4 OZ	7 G
1/3 OZ	10 G
1/2 OZ	14 G
1 OZ	28 G
2 OZ	57 G
3 OZ	85 G
4 OZ	113 G
5 OZ	142 G
6 OZ	170 G
7 OZ	198 G
8 OZ	227 G
9 OZ	255 G
10 OZ	284 G
11 OZ	312 G
12 OZ	340 G
13 OZ	369 G
14 OZ	397 G
15 OZ	425 G
16 OZ	454 G

Oven Temperatures

300°F	150°C
325°F	165°C
350°F	180°C
375°F	190°C
400°F	200°C
425°F	220°C
450°F	230°C
475°F	245°C

Helpful Formulas

Tablespoons x 14.79 = Milliliters
Cups x 0.236 = Liters
Ounces x 28.35 = Grams
Degrees F – 32 x 5 ÷ 9 = Degrees C
Inches x 2.54 = Centimeters

Made in the USA
Monee, IL
17 June 2020

34054044R00040